AF255596

TREES

A Photographic Study in Determination

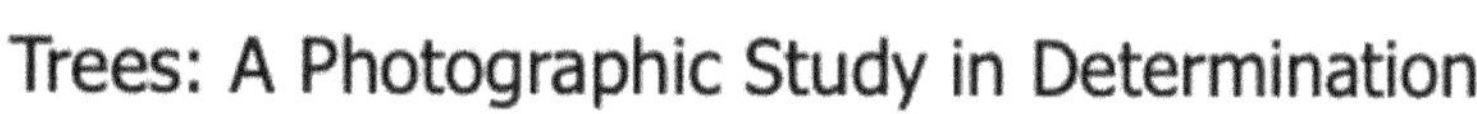

Pinyon Mountain Studios

Reno, NV 89521

Trees: A Photographic Study in Determination

Copyright 2026 – All Rights Reserved

Photographic prints are available at
https://pinyonmtnstudios.artstorefronts.com

info@pinyonmtnstudios.com

Published by Pinyon Mountain Studios through Marketing and Publishing House, LLC

ISBN: 978-1-969818-52-3

All work in this book is the work of the author and is not to be reproduced without the express written consent by the same.

Foreword to *Trees: A Photographic Study in Determination*

Inspiring, remarkable, and profoundly moving, this collection is a beautiful photographic interpretation of determination by an exceptionally talented photographer and an equally remarkable human being.

In *Trees*, Dana Garrett has chosen a subject that at first glance seems simple. Yet through his lens, trees become powerful symbols of resilience. His extraordinary assortment of trees from around the world reveals the arduous journey of growth, roots gripping rock, trunks bending with the wind, and branches reaching relentlessly toward light. Each image speaks of strength. Each photograph whispers determination.

What makes this body of work so compelling is not only the subject matter, but the way Dana sees. In black and white, distractions disappear. What remains is form, texture, contrast, and truth. The stark interplay of light and shadow mirrors the challenges these trees have endured and ultimately overcome.

These are not merely photographs of trees. They are portraits of perseverance.

As photographers, we understand that capturing an image is about far more than pressing a shutter. It requires patience, awareness, and the ability to recognize a story when it quietly reveals itself. Dana has done just that. He has given us images that invite reflection not just on nature, but on our own lives.
I am confident you will find yourself lingering over each photograph and its story. And perhaps, in the quiet strength of these trees, you will discover renewed strength within your own soul to continue the journey we call life.

Sincerely,
Lou Manna
Commercial Photographer (30 years)
Former *New York Times* Photojournalist (15 years)

Dedicated to Stephen Colbert & Crew

This is a portfolio of trees I have found growing in difficult conditions, yet somehow seemed to be thriving. Since you learned of the cancellation of your show this coming May 2026, you have been like the trees I have sought out to capture. In each show, you have demonstrated determination and grace in continuing despite difficult circumstances.

I have long been a fan of your show and enjoy your monologues and selection of guests.

I am a retired Navy Chief Petty Officer and was a meteorologist and oceanographer. I was the Chief Meteorologist for three different amphibious assault ships and three different Marine Expeditionary Units. I also served as the Officer of the Deck (Underway) on each ship, served as the Officer of the Deck (Underway) on each ship, served as a Combat Information Center Watch Officer (CICWO), was member of the Damage Control Training Team (DCTT), and as DCTT Coordinator.

To say this was a "tough gig" is an understatement, but I loved every aspect of what I did in executing my mission and that of the ship.

That you have a tough gig putting together a show every night to make people laugh while presenting serious content is not lost on me.

Therefore, I present to you the first copy of my photographic collection on this subject: Determination. I know you will complete your mission with dignity, integrity, and grace. I retired in 2014 because I was no longer able to go back to sea. The Navy made the decision for me. Therefore, I think I am uniquely qualified to say I understand what happened to you.

I miss it every day, as you will miss your show every day. I sincerely hope the network pulls its collective head out of its unwashed backside and reinstates your show.

If they don't, then I wish you Fair Winds and Following Seas.

BRAVO ZULU!

Very Respectfully,
Dana Garrett, Photographer
Pinyon Mountain Studios

Introduction

Trees: A Photographic Study in Determination is a portfolio of photographs that succinctly depict the struggle to survive in harsh, difficult conditions. I have an affinity for this subject as I see it as a metaphor for not just my life's history, but the life histories of millions who have worked, sweat, face seemingly insurmountable hardships, and yet are still surviving, even thriving in the landscape of their lives.

I have been in love with the outdoors since my earliest years. Walking among the giants of the forests, I have always found a sense of tranquility and peace. Seeing trees growing in the conditions and landscapes depicted within my work only serves to strengthen my resolve to continue forward, even during my darkest days.

I am a retired Navy Chief Petty Officer and was an enlisted meteorologist / oceanographer. I served 4 years in the U.S. Air Force in this capacity. For three years after, I was in the Air Force Reserve in Combat Telecommunications, and in 1984, shipped over to the Navy Reserve to return to meteorology. I spent the next 15 years in this capacity, earning the rank of Senior Chief and being selected for one of the greatest and most difficult jobs: to be a Command Senior Chief. In 1998, an opportunity to return to active service in the Navy appeared, and I took it. In January of 1999, after my 40th birthday, I was returned to active duty, provided I accepted an administrative reduction in rank back to Chief Petty Officer. I did so willingly.

Fast forward to 2013. I was completing a shore tour assignment and was being tasked to take orders back to sea duty. I would have done so willingly, but in the intervening years, I had racked up more than a few medical and physical difficulties. The Sea Screening Doc asked me if I wanted to go back to sea. I said without hesitation, "Yes". He was surprised by this. Then he asked if I thought I should. I told him that was a whole 'nother ball of worms. Given my arthritis and back and joint pain, I said it was probably not a good idea. So, of the three categories, I was marked Unsuitable.

Within a week or so, I received a message from the Navy that since I had been found Unsuitable for sea duty, I was no longer deployable worldwide. As a result, I had ten days (nine, actually, as I received the message a day late) to apply for retirement effective 1 March 2014, or be administratively separated. This meant no retirement pay or benefits to me.

My request for retirement was processed post-haste, and I retired honorably on 1 March 2014. To say being forced to retire was a gut punch is not overstating the situation. I have been retired for over 12 years now, and I still have not gotten used to it.

So how does Stephen Colbert and *The Late Show* fit into all of this? When I heard in 2025 that his show was being canceled by CBS, via collusion and a $16 million payout to our government, I felt the same gut punch.
It was Stephen's commitment to continue his show with integrity, dignity, and grace that sparked the idea for this

book. Stephen and his crew were facing a deadline to "retire". I had the same experience. Trees have always had a dignity and grace to me, especially those I had discovered in less-than-optimal conditions. SO, the idea of creating a photo book of this subject and dedicating it to Stephen Colbert and *the Late Show* crew seemed a good idea.
So here we are. I sincerely hope this book of photos demonstrating surviving and thriving through the hardships life throws at the creatures, and by extension "us," helps to show that just because life is difficult, we can still carry on with dignity, grace, and integrity.

Dana Garrett

TREES

A Photographic Study in Determination

A Portfolio
By
Dana Garrett

Morning at Tenaya Lake

The pines lean forward into the morning light

as dawn comes to Tenaya Lake in the Yosemite High Country.

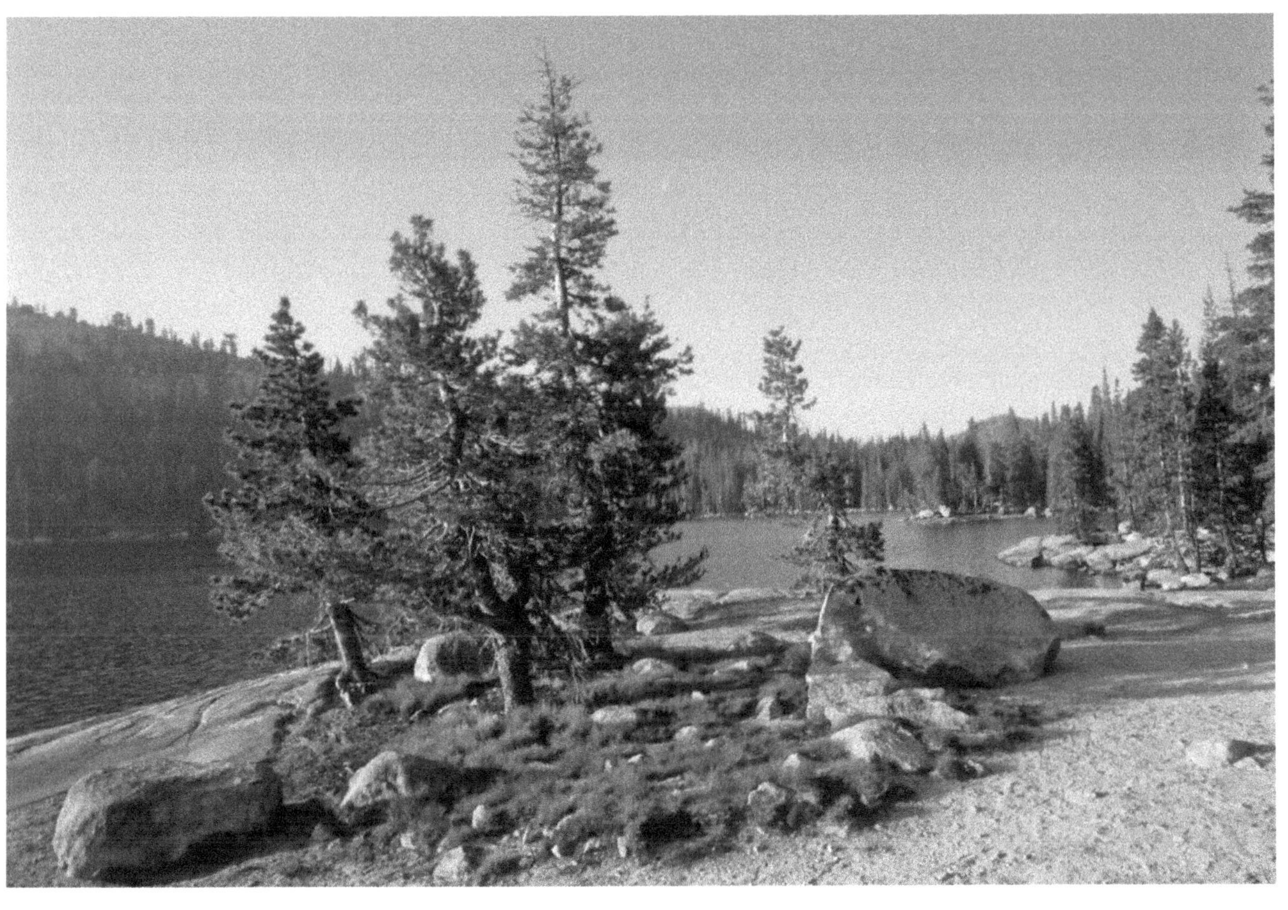

Bent but Not Broken

This Monterey Cypress (Cupressus macrocarpa) is an old trail marker tree. Native Americans would bend young trees in this manner to mark their trails. This one is quite old, and is located at Point Lobos State Reserve, south ofCarmel by the Sea.

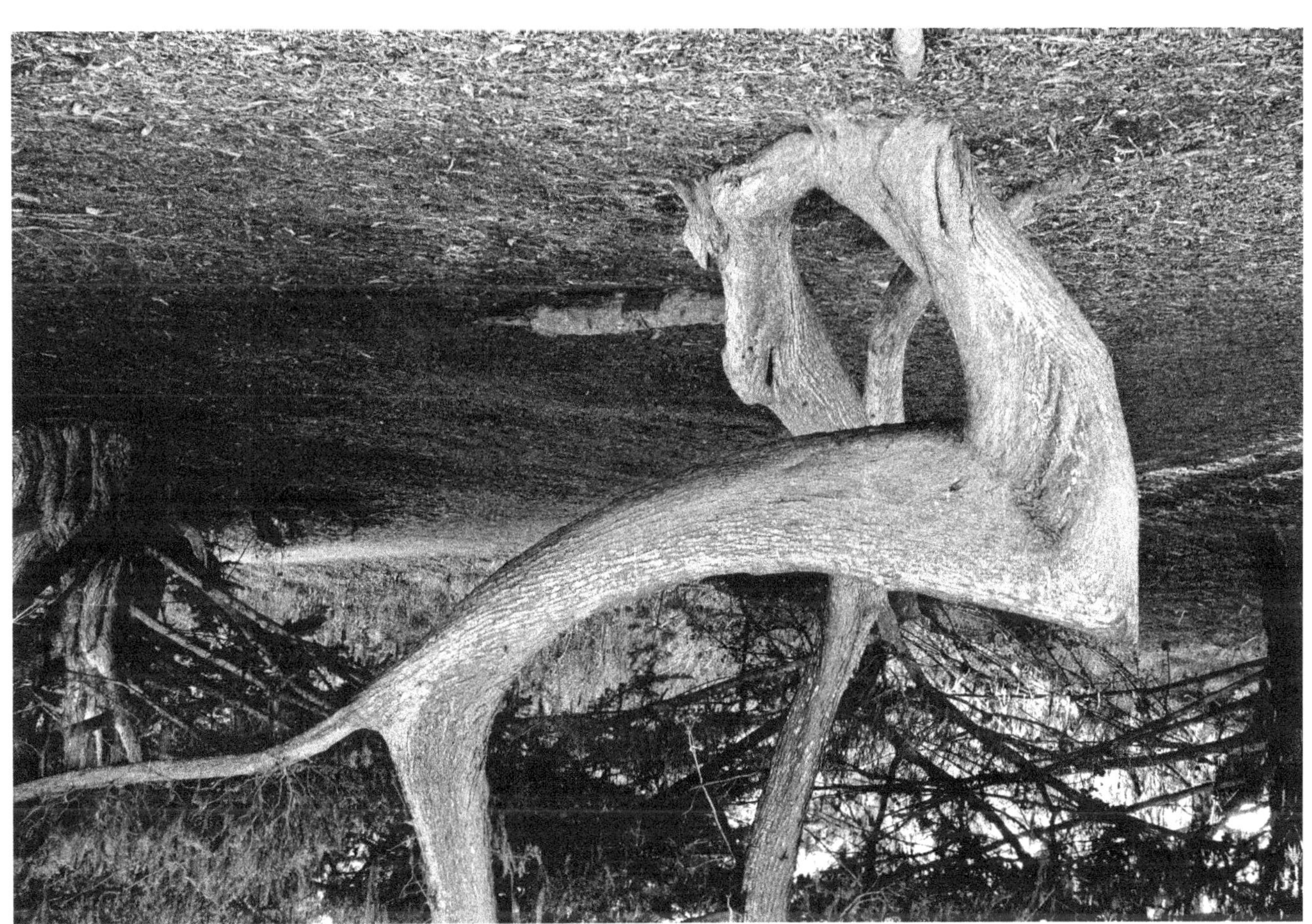

Stone Olive

This Olive tree (Olea europaea) had taken on the color ofthe red clay dirt around it. It looked as ifit had been molded from the clay itself, taken at sunset in Crete near Governeto Monastery.

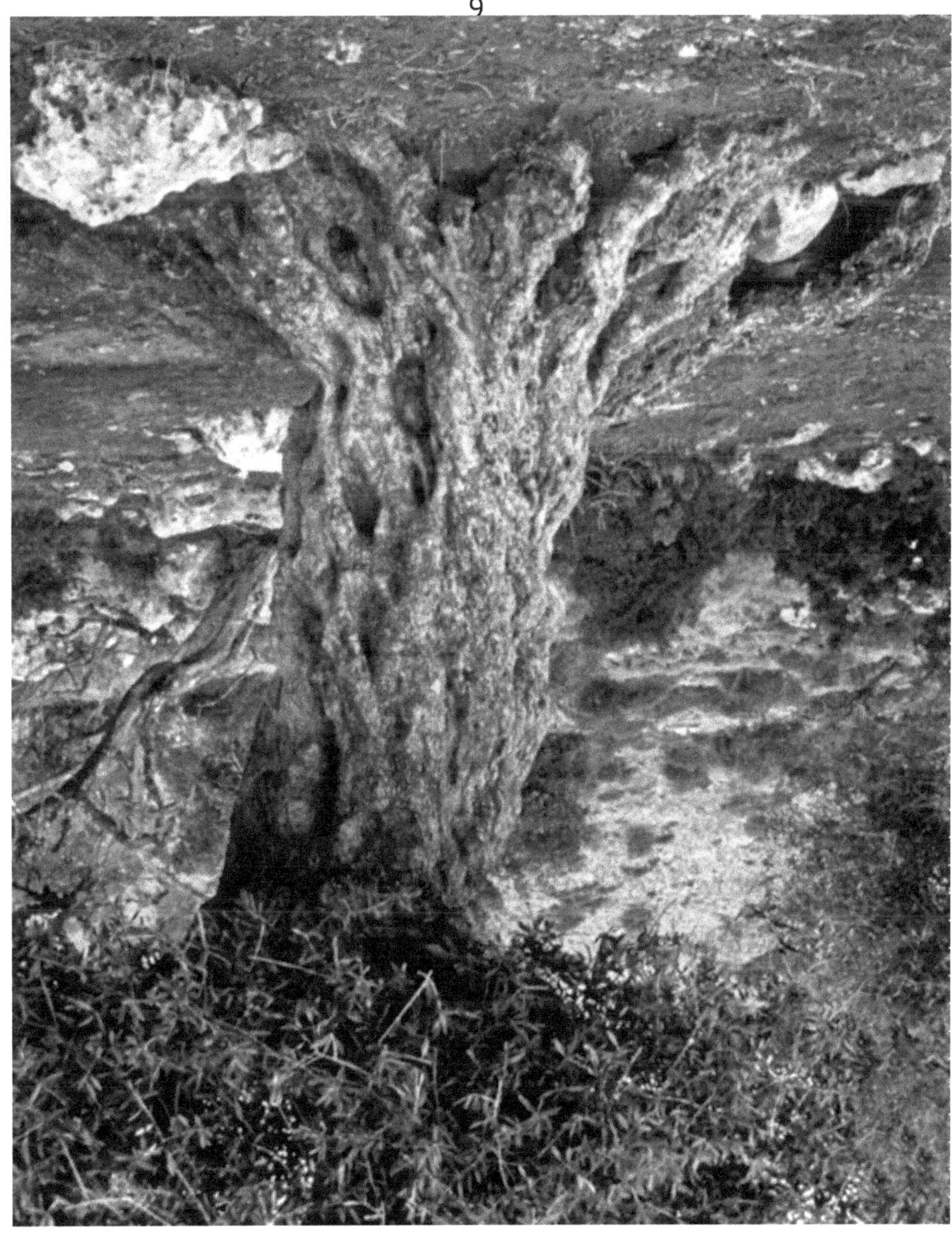

Mammoth Cypress

*This huge Bald Cypress (Taxodium distichum) tree is its own island
in Powhatan Creek, Williamsburg, VA.*

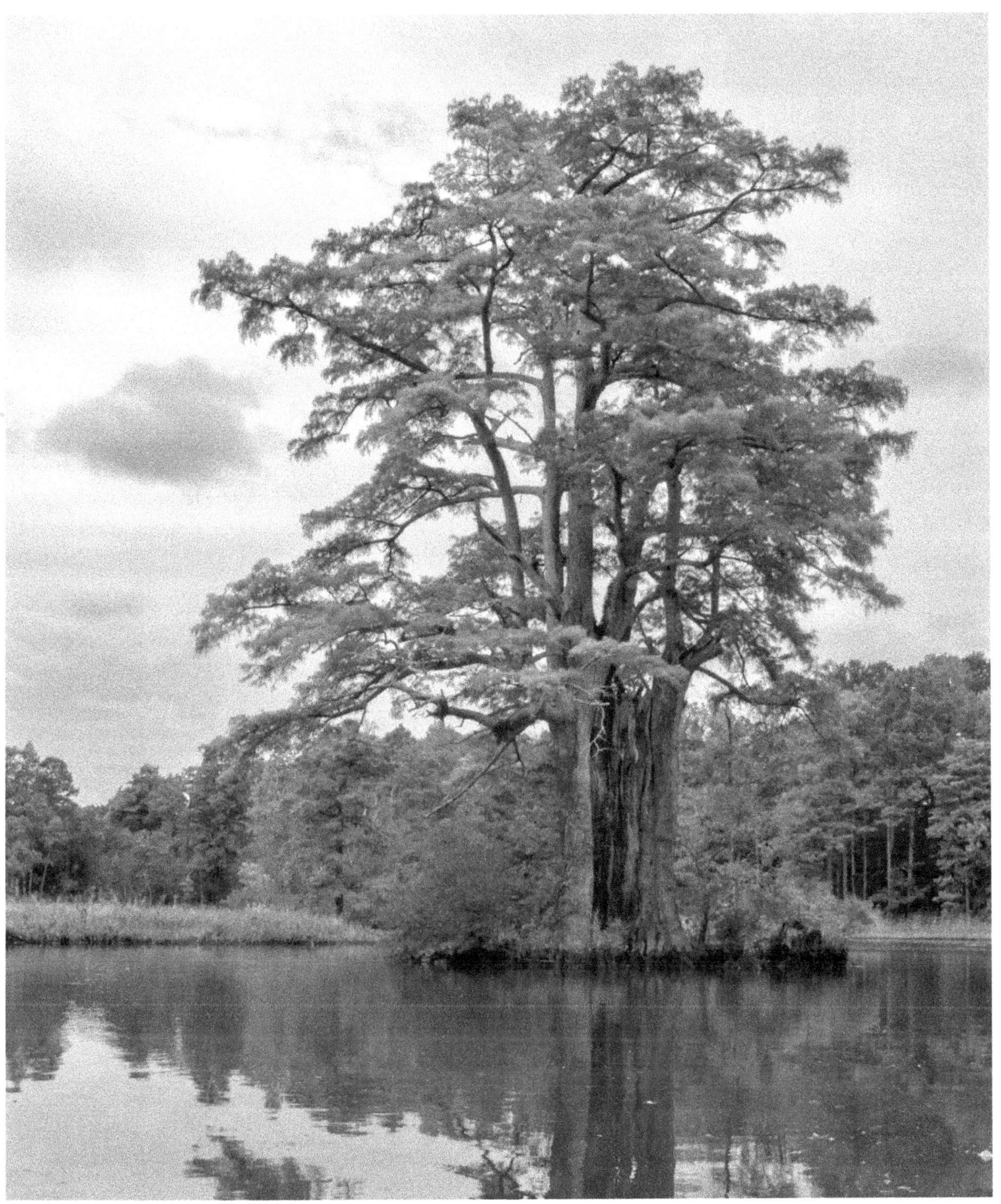

Lone Cypress at Point Lobos

This lone Monterey Cypress (Cupressus macrocarpa) at Point Lobos State Reserve is located on this rocky point, visible from the parking lot where the Allen Memorial Grove Trail, the Cypress Grove Trail, and the Sea Lion Point Trails meet. It is one ofthe most elegant trees I have ever seen.

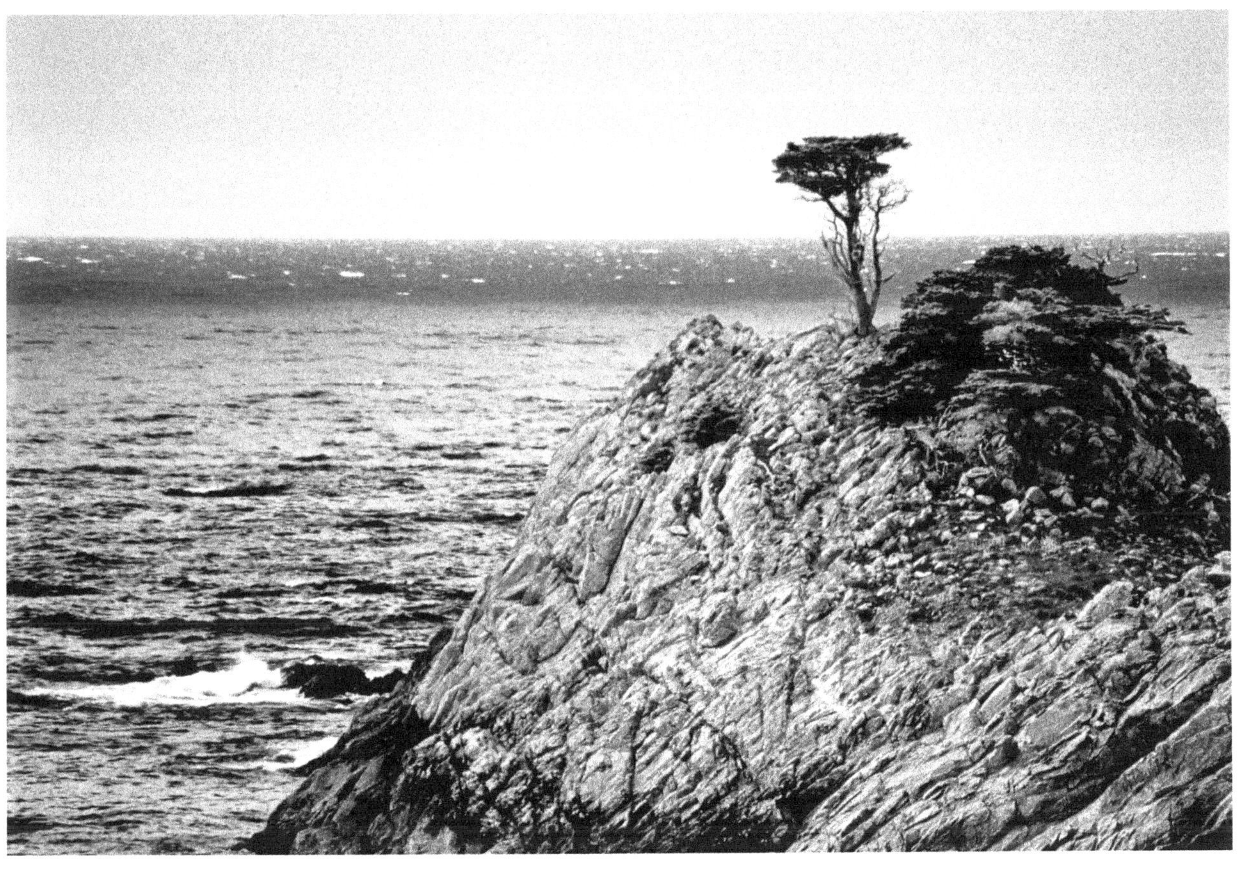

Gnarled Oak

This Coastal Live Oak tree (Quercus agrifolia) had some ofthe most twisted branches I have ever seen on a coastal live oak (Quercus agrifolia), taken in Gilroy, CA.

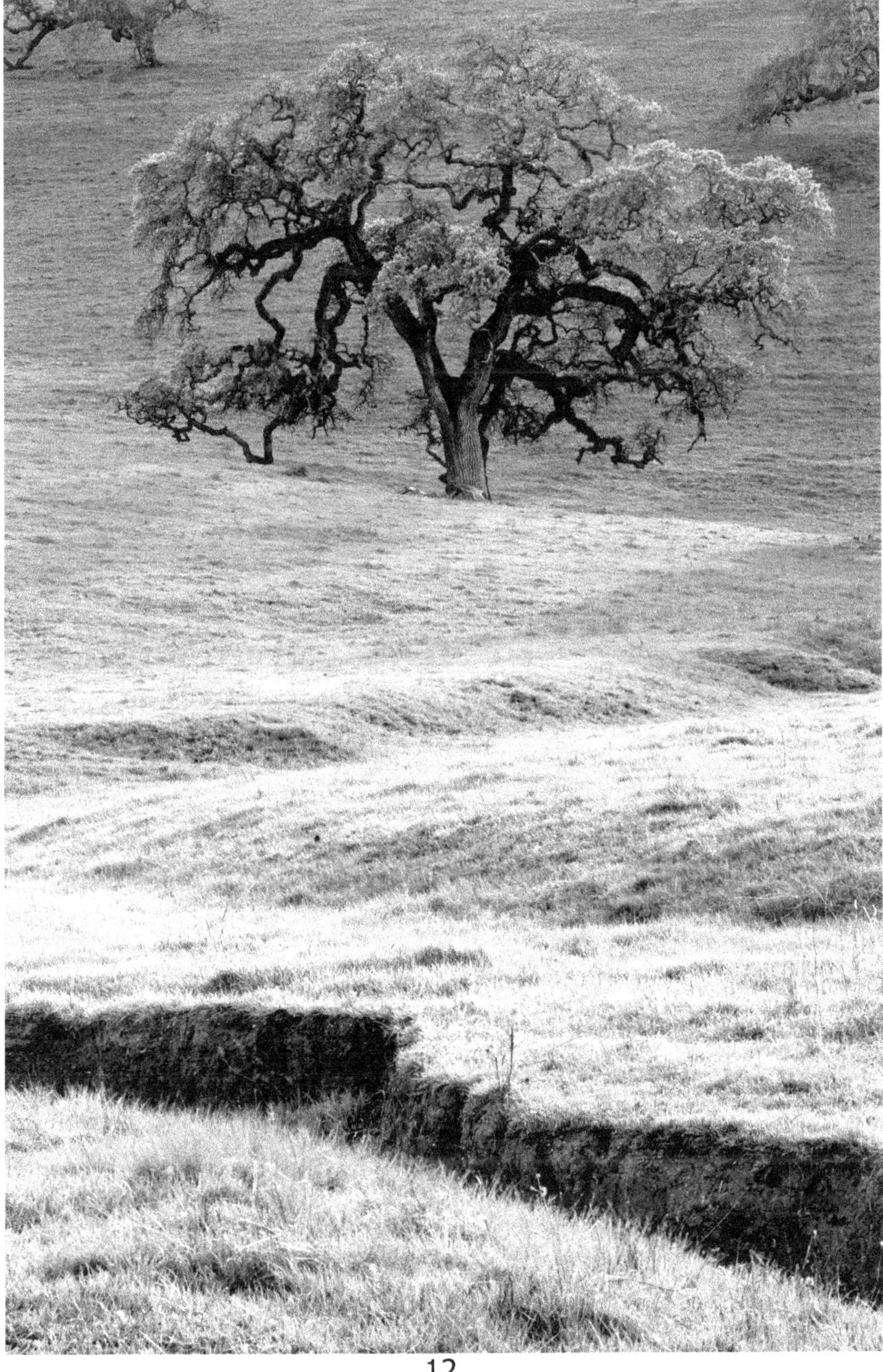

Determination

This is the most impressive display I have seen ofnature taking its course. This tree root had split the stone in trying to get to the soil in the Imbros Gorge in southern Crete, Greece.

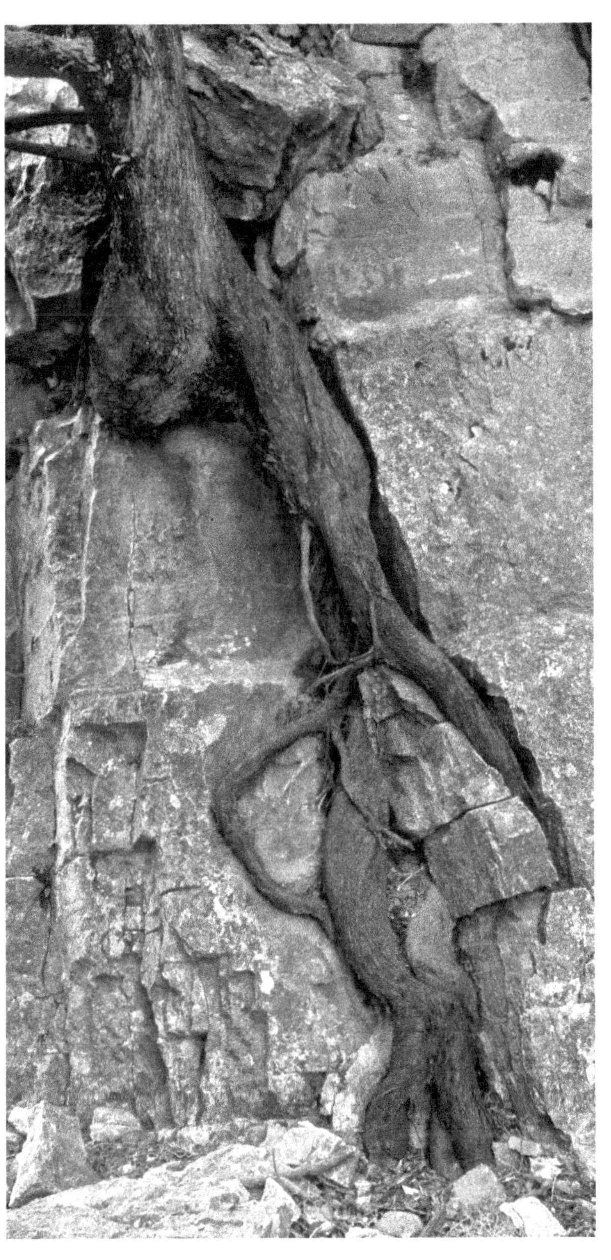

Between a Rock and a Highway

I have watched this Ponderosa pine (Pinus ponderosa) grow in this impossible location on the lower Geiger Grade highway in Reno, NV for 12 years now. It is incredible that it survives here.

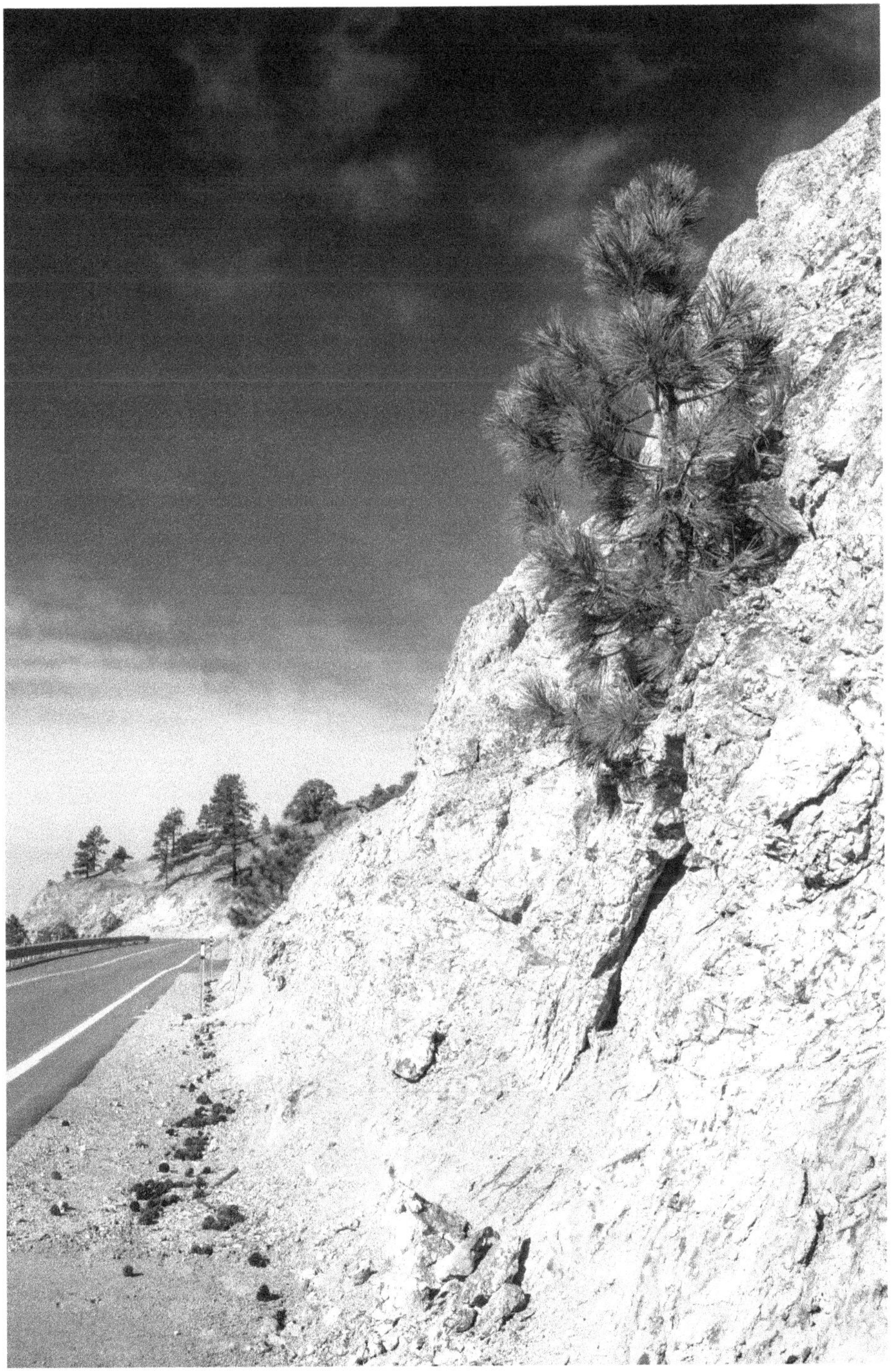

Last of Their Kind

Trees are not common in Crete. The island has been significantly deforested, and thorny shrubs have grown in their place. These two trees, located near Theriso, Crete struck me as out of place and something to be remembered. Crete has since begun a tree planting program to reverse the deforestation.

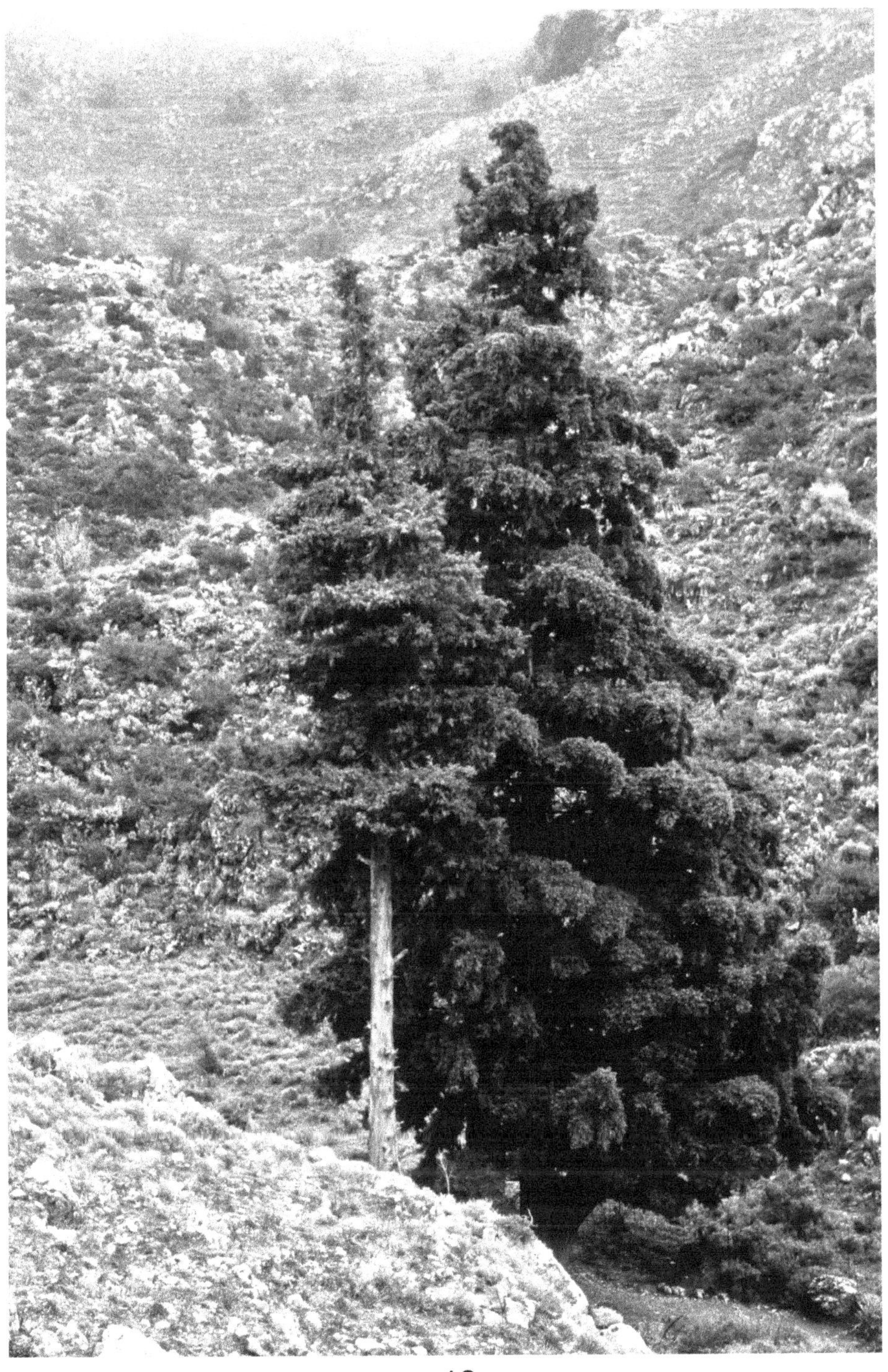

Lone Pinyon Pine

This Pinyon Pine (Pinus monophylla) is growing along a ridge in the Virginia Mountains southeast ofReno, Nevada. The Eastern Sierra Carson Range is visible in the background.

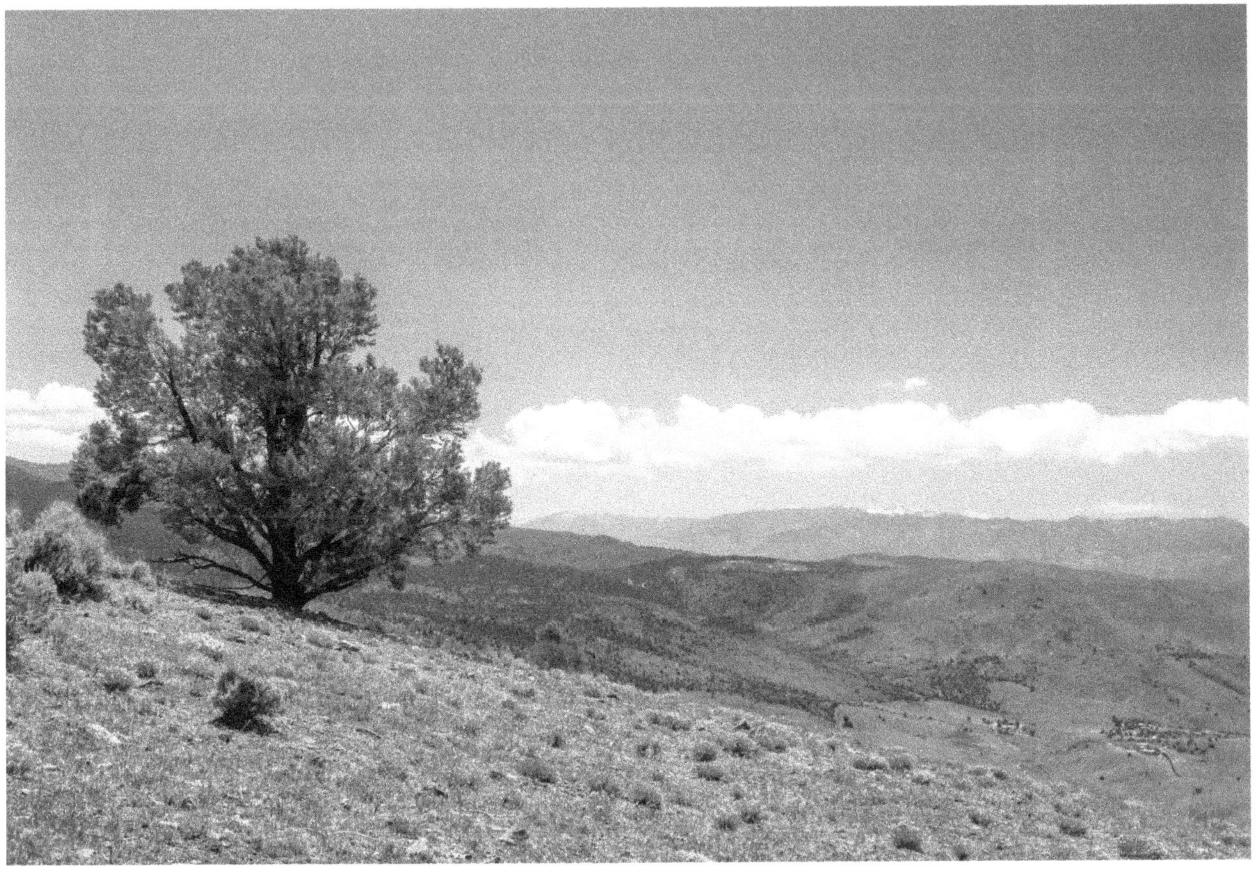

Standing Against the Wind

This Ponderosa pine (Pinus ponderosa) is near the Slide Mountain Ski Area in the Eastern Sierra. The branches are all pointing to the east because ofthe strong mountain winds.

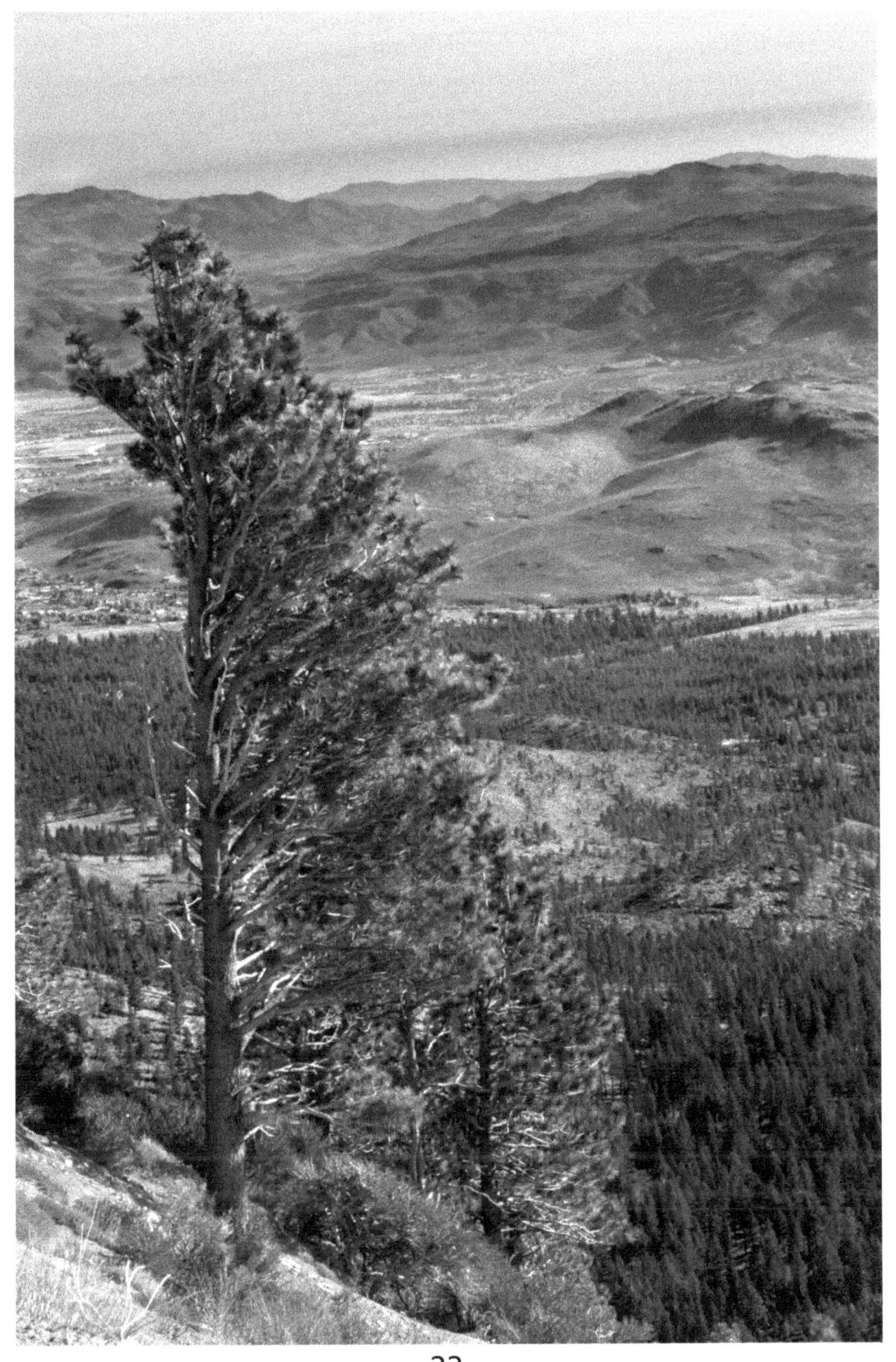

Stunted Lodgepole

This Lodgepole pine (Pinus contorta) is growing on a rocky ridge high in the Eastern Sierra. Subjected to fiercely high winds, these trees fight a losing battle against the elements. Yet still, they grow.

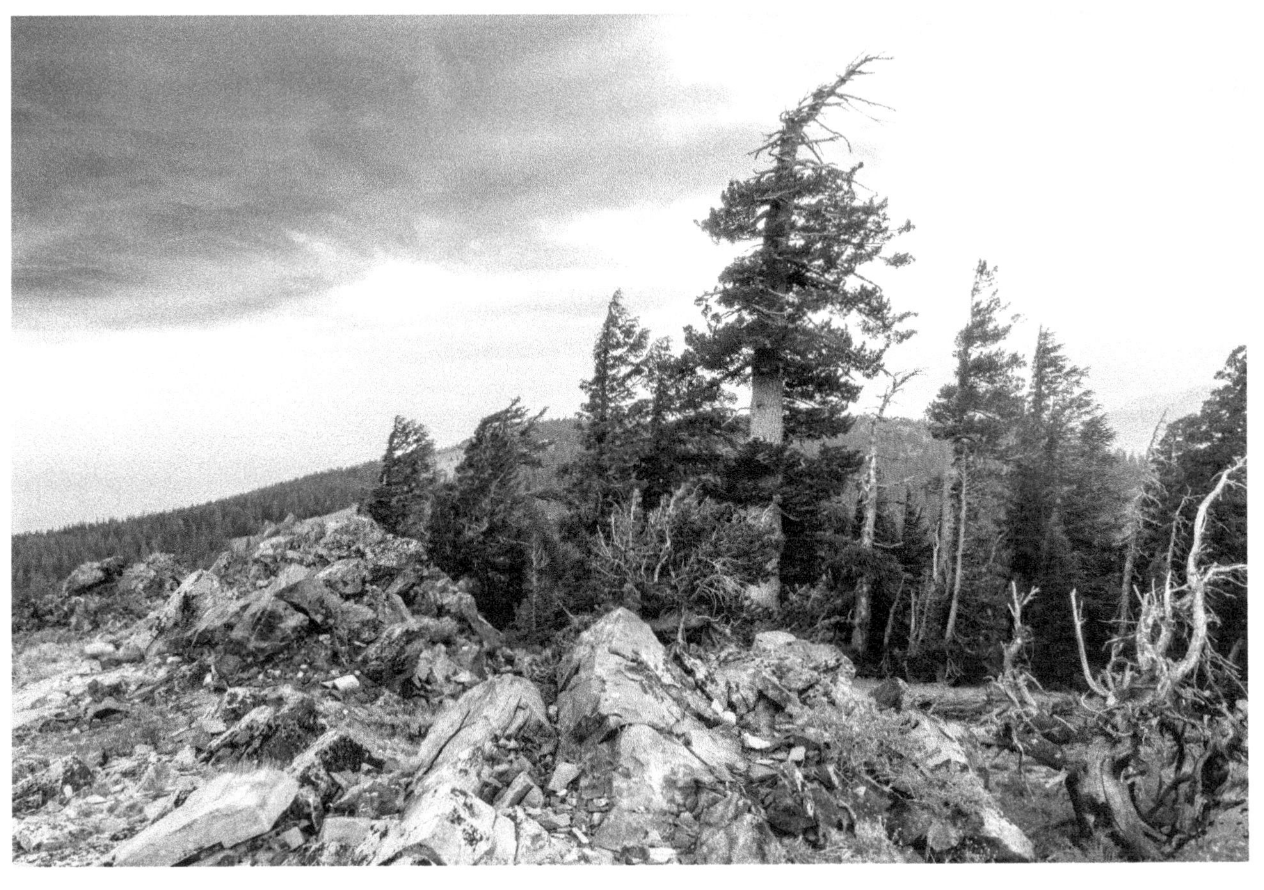

Not Forgotten

Looking like the aftermath ofa WWI battlefield, these trees are dormant in December as the fog settles on Kallergi mountain in the Lefka Ori (White Mountains), on the island ofCrete, near the head ofthe Samaria Gorge and the Omalos Plain.

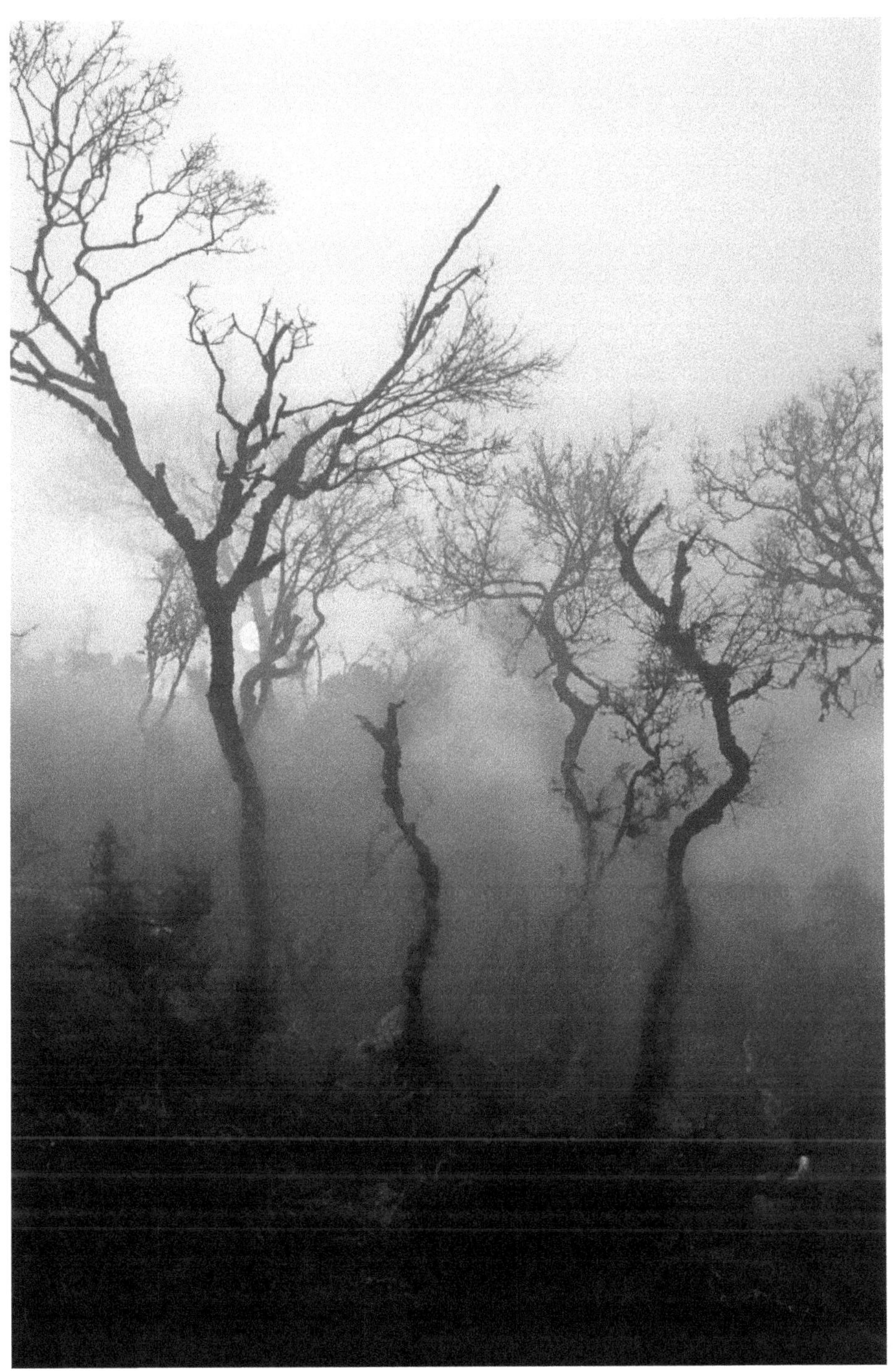

Sprawling Roots

This Ponderosa pine (Pinus ponderosa) growing on the side ofthe Geiger Grade in Reno, NV has three major roots on the surface holding this tree in place. The root in the front actually broke through the rock covering it. The trees are tough and determined to grow in inhospitable soil and rock.

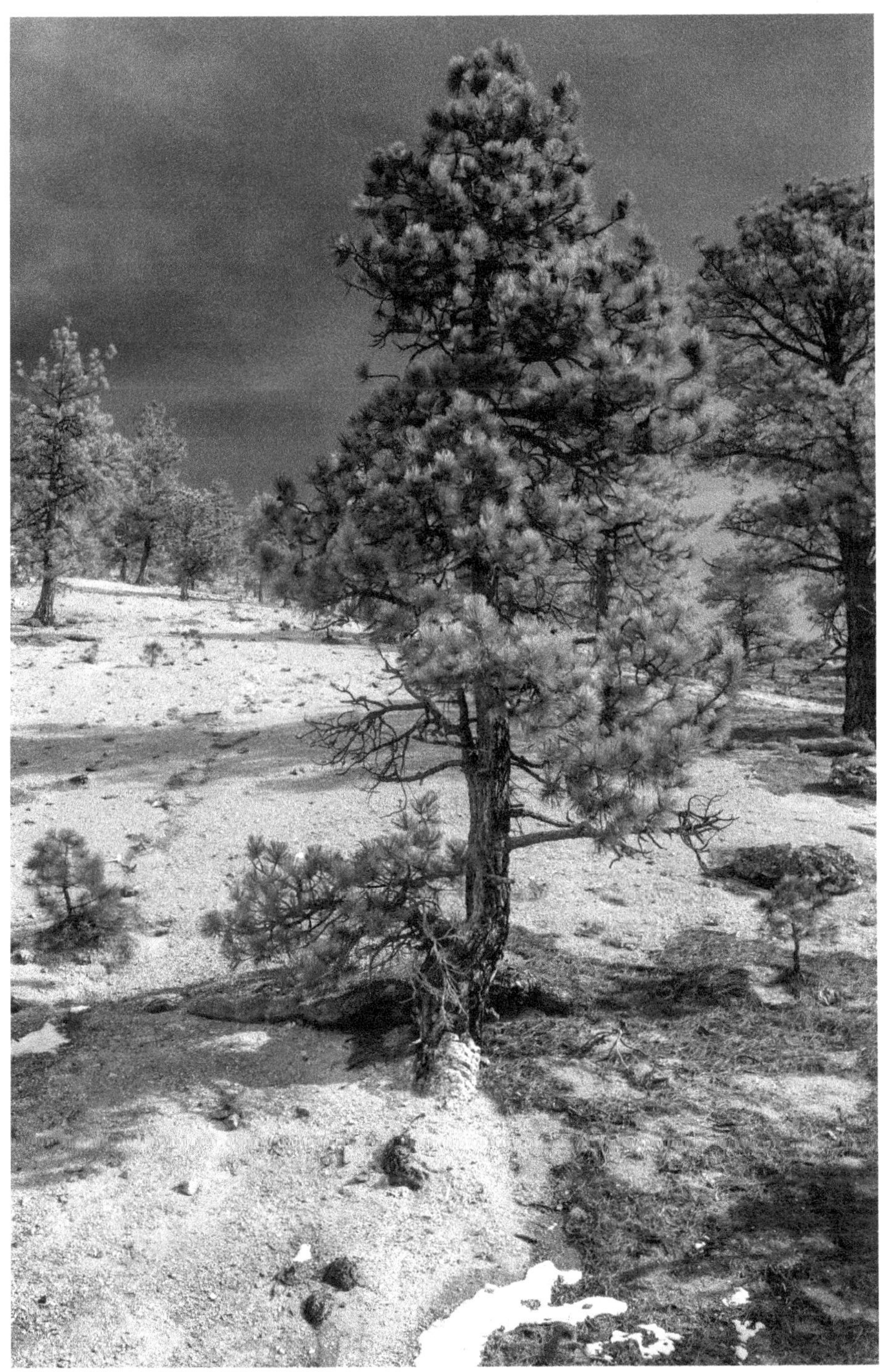

Stone and Oak

I went to Castle Rock State Park in northern California with a friend who was into rock climbing and bouldering. I was struck by this gigantic oak growing from underneath these enormous boulders. If you look closely, the boulder in front looks like a dog's head sniffing the tree.

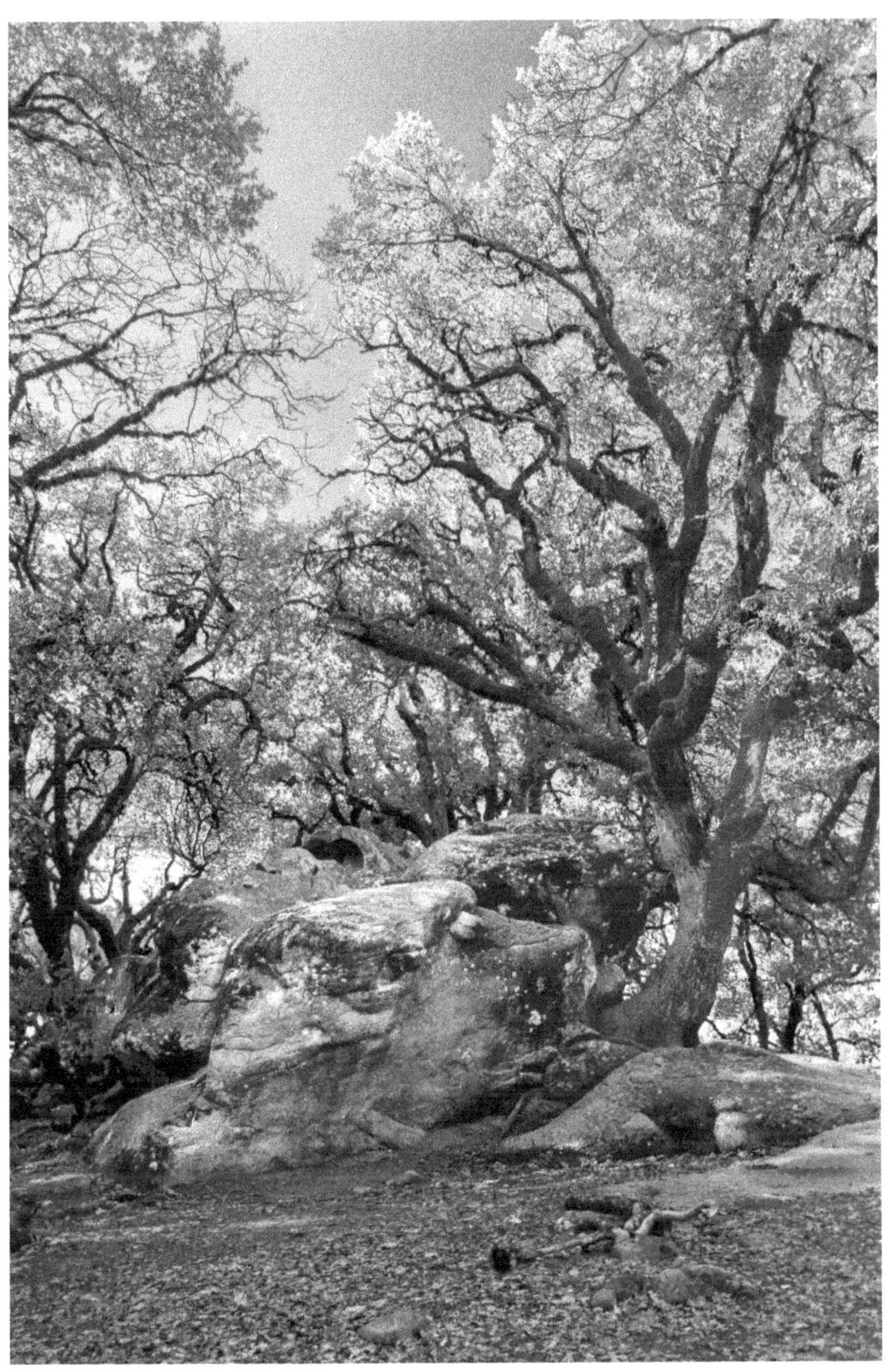

Ancient

This Juniper (Juniperus occidentalis) in the high country in Yosemite was ancient by anyone's standards and was still growing.

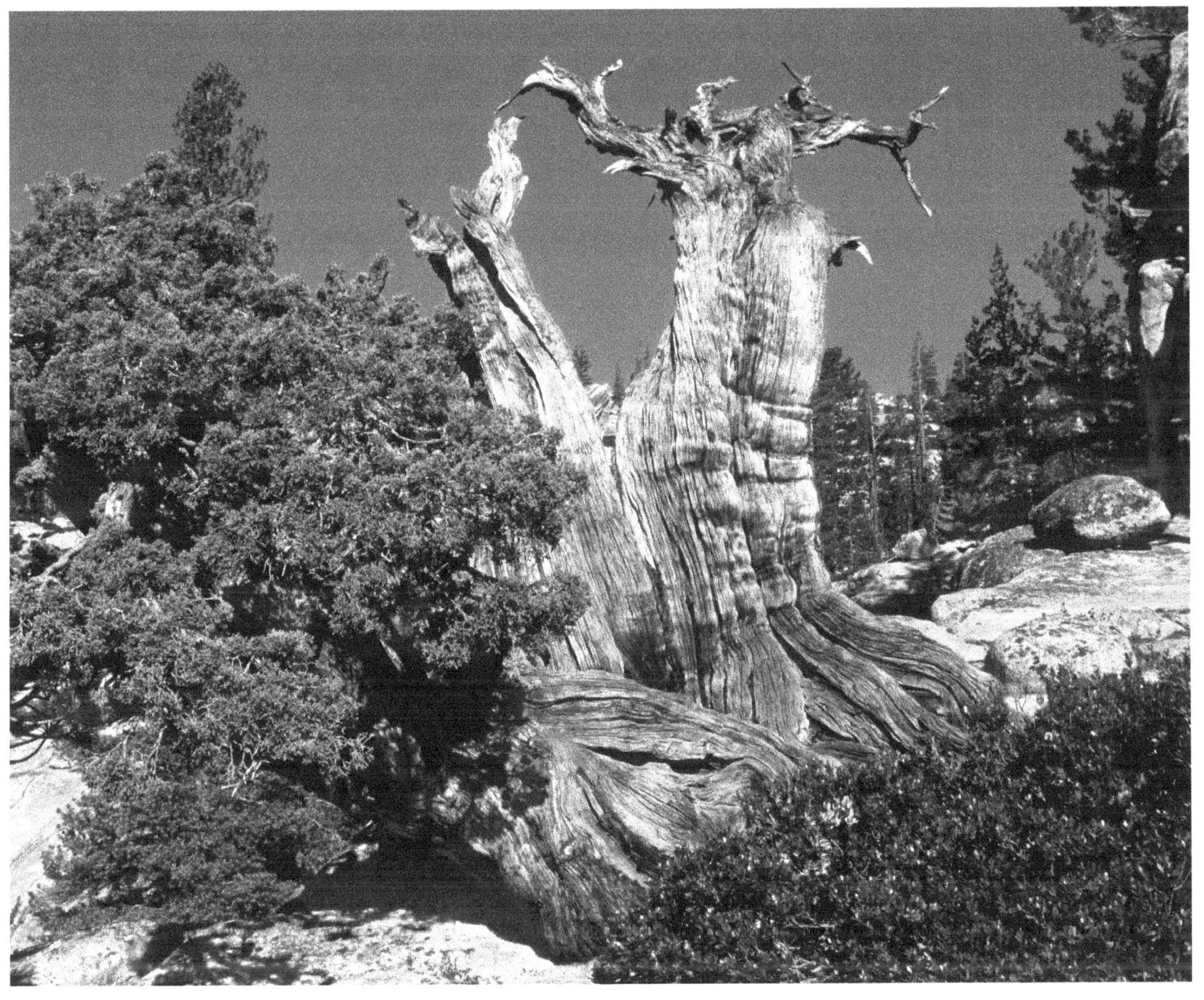

Hanging On

The mountain slopes along the Geiger Grade are populated with Ponderosa pine trees (Pinus ponderosa). The landscape is so harsh, most ofthem are stunted in their growth and do not rise to their full height and size, as can be seen across the valley in the Sierra. Yet they persist.

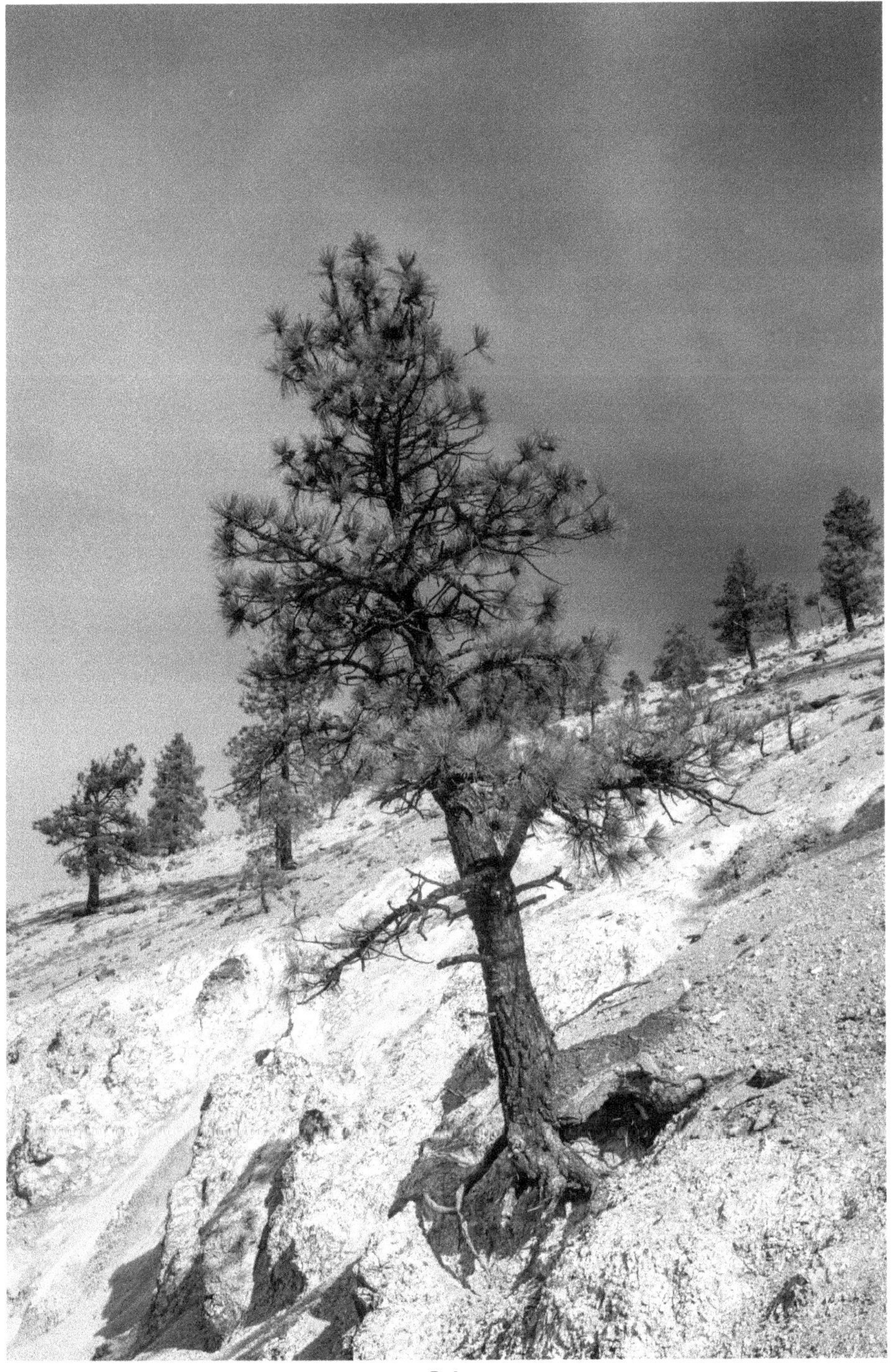

Perseverance

There are many pine trees in the Virginia Range that defy the landscape and grow any way they can. This Ponderosa Pine (Pinus ponderosa) is no exception. This tree is growing vertically out ofa large horizontal trunk/root on this hillside.

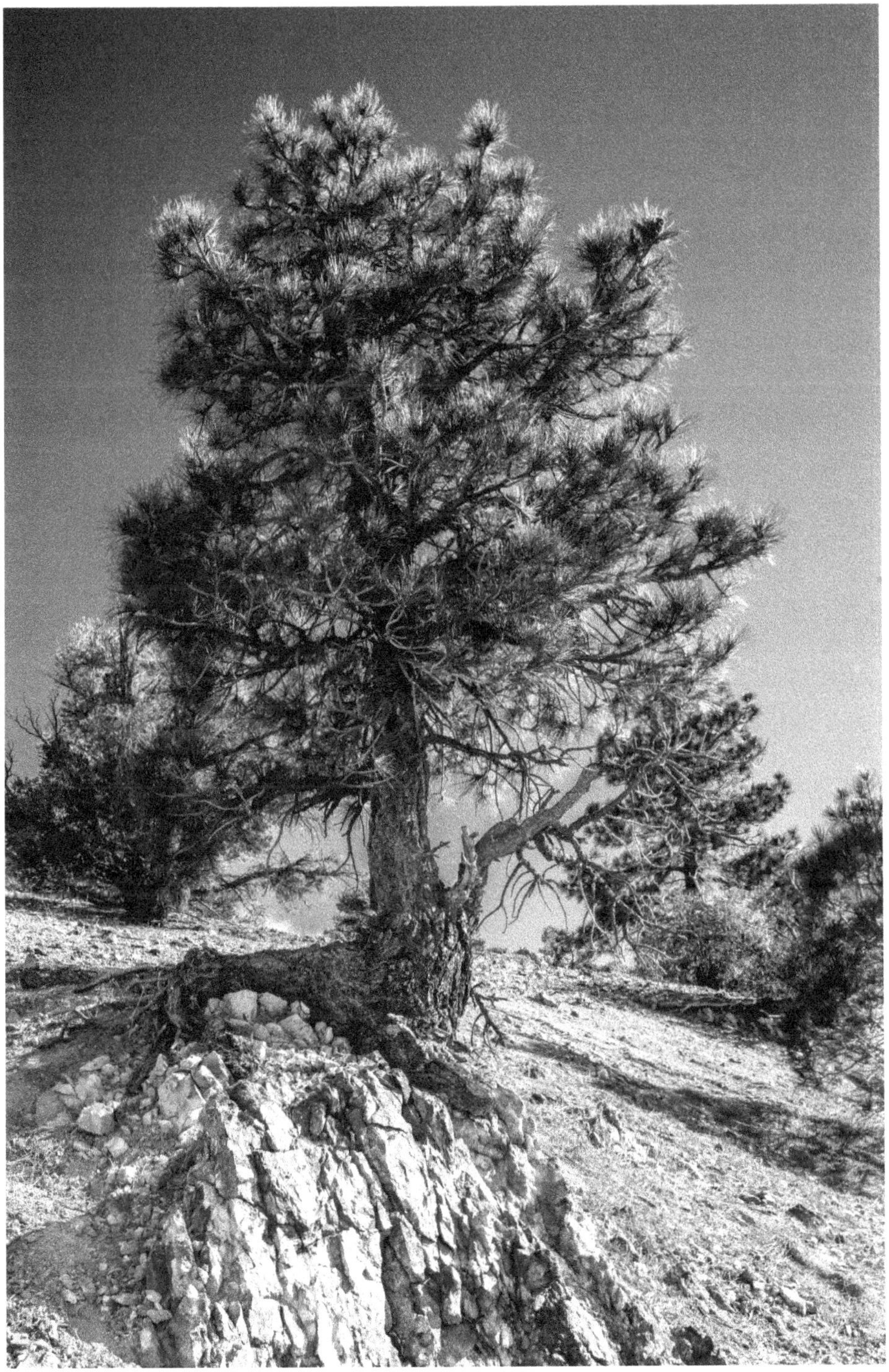

Long Stretch

This stunted Ponderosa pine (Pinus ponderosa) located above the Geiger Grade in Reno, NV stretched one ofits major roots a long way to find sustenance on this barren hillside.

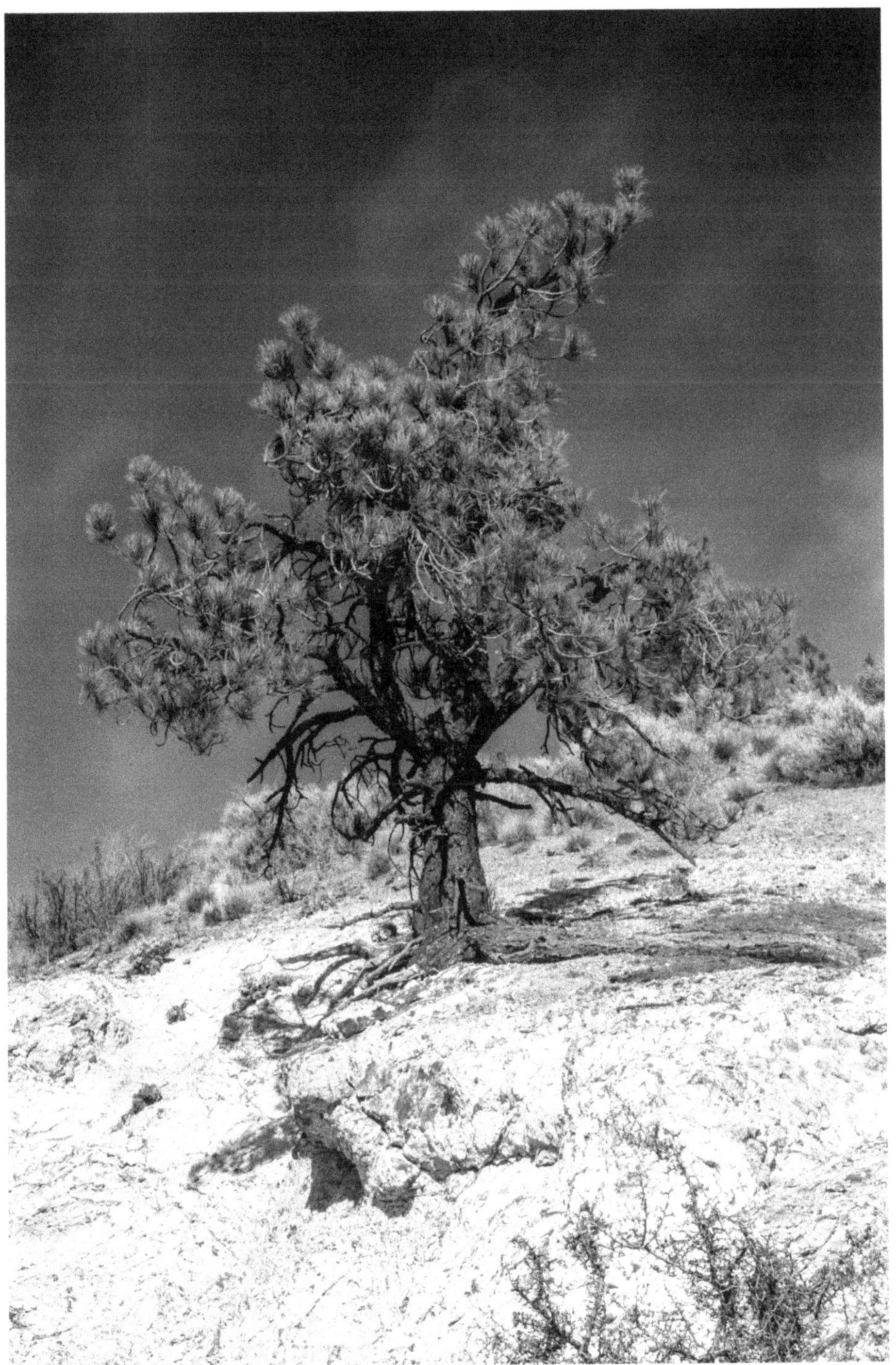

Struggling to Survive

The Ponderosa pines (Pinus ponderosa) that grow along the Geiger Grade are mostly stunted in size. This one appears to be having a harder time ofit, yet it still lives.

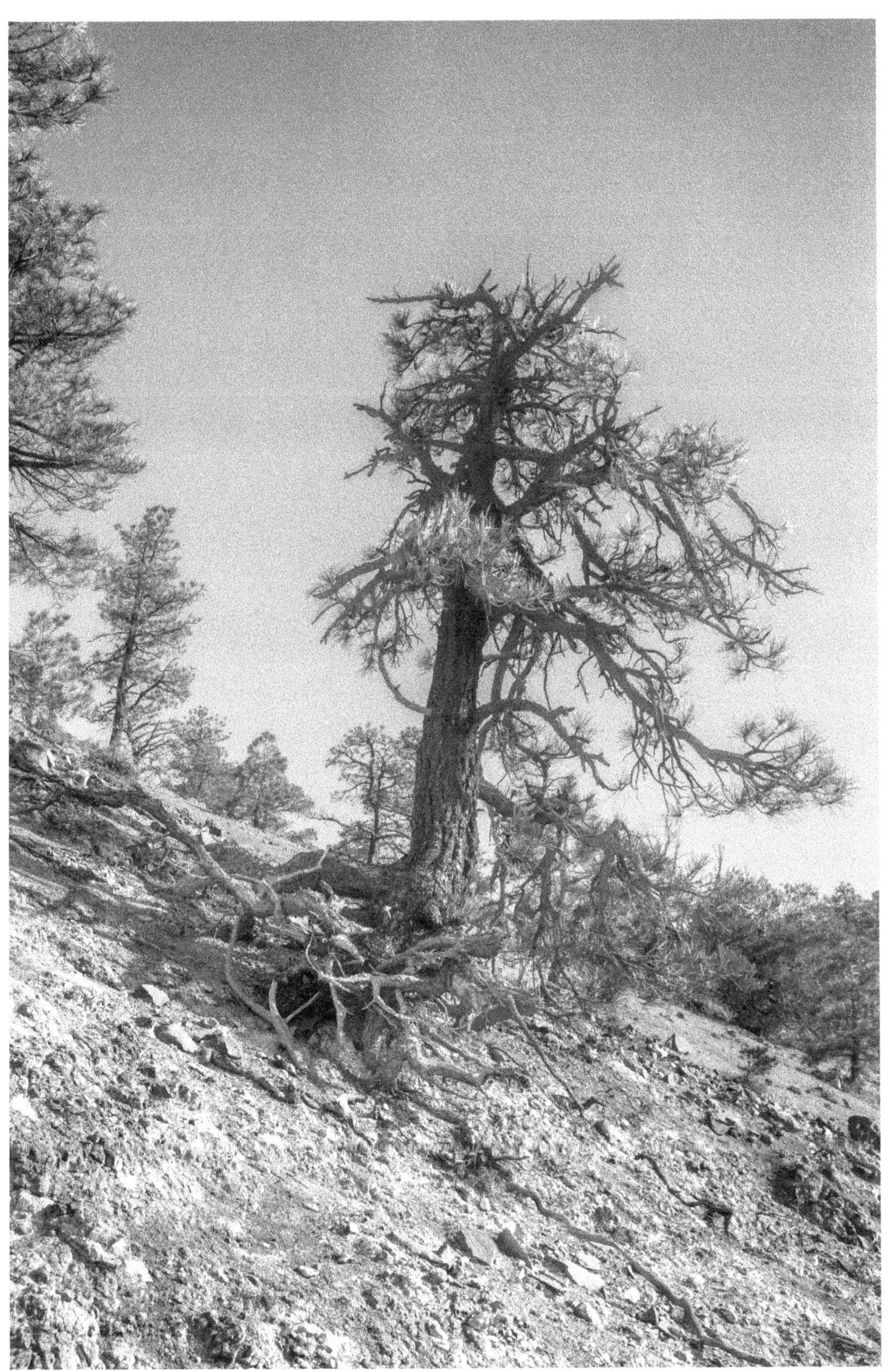

It's Tough Growing Up

This struggling alpine pine tree and the boulder next to it reminded me ofwhat it was like growing up in tough neighborhoods. Cathedral Peak is in the upper left corner.

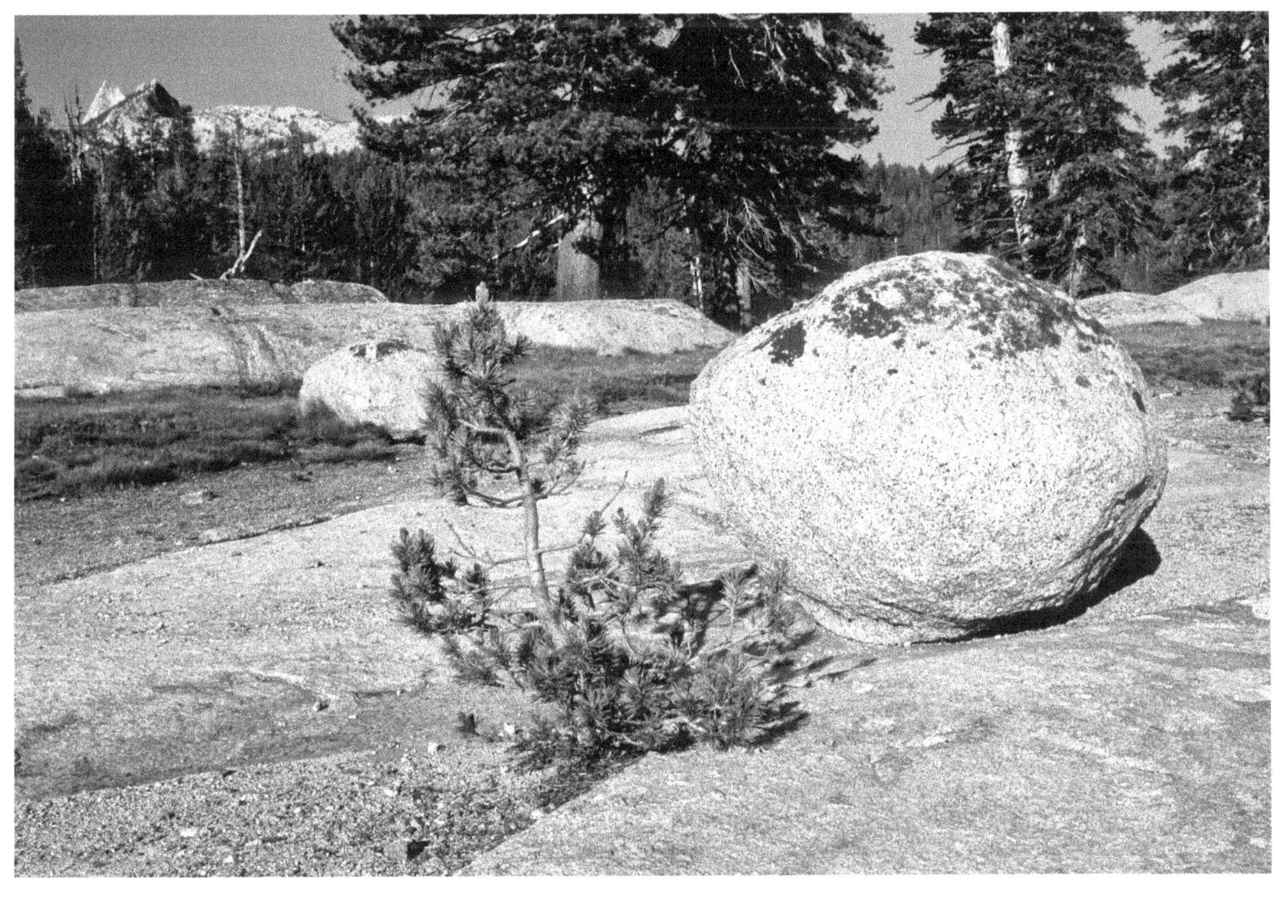

Sunset Pine

These pines are on top ofthe cliffs above Tunnel View on the Wawona Road. I was there just as the sun was setting, and this pine tree just lit up as ifit were ablaze from the setting sun.

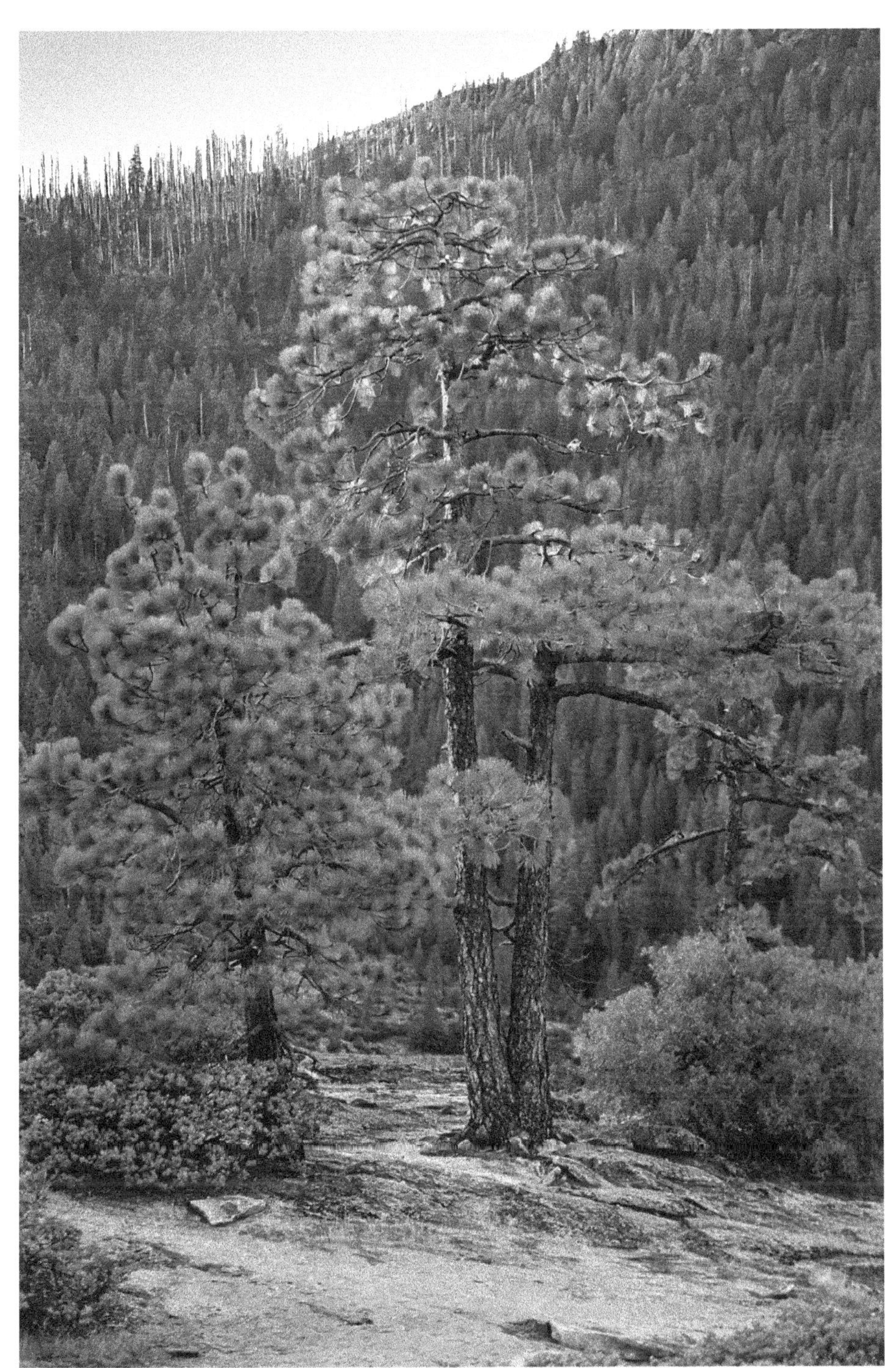

Tree with a View

This is another Ponderosa pine (Pinus ponderosa) growing in a sparse location above the Geiger Grade and is stunted in its growth. But it has a spectacular view ofthe Eastern Sierra.

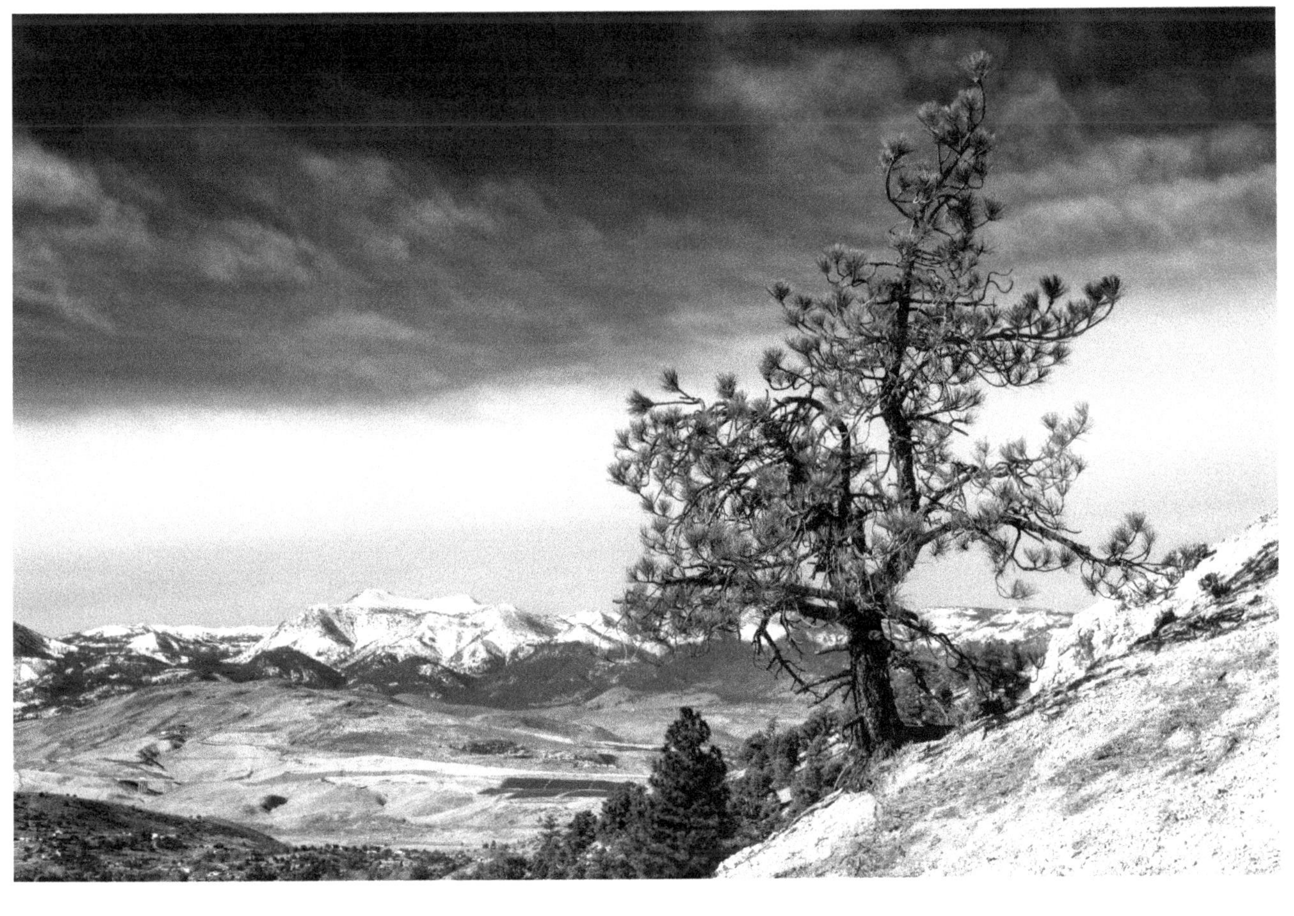

Artist's Statement

Trees: A Photographic Study in Determination explores the intricate relationship between resilience and the natural world, particularly through the lens of trees in various landscapes. Utilizing black-and-white photography, the artist captures the stark beauty of these enduring forms, revealing their character and strength against the elements. Each piece serves as a meditation on survival, showcasing trees that stand alone or in clusters, often in challenging environments.

I am driven by a fascination with the stories that trees tell—how they adapt, endure, and thrive despite adversity. This exploration is influenced by my deep appreciation for nature and its ability to evoke a sense of tranquility and reflection. I find the monochromatic palette enhances the textures and contrasts within each scene, inviting viewers to contemplate the interplay of light and shadow, as well as the emotional resonance of solitude and perseverance.

Through this collection, I try to convey a powerful message about resilience, encouraging viewers to reflect on their own experiences of struggle and triumph. The trees, with their gnarled branches and steadfast roots, embody a spirit of determination that resonates universally. This work not only celebrates the beauty of the natural world but also serves as a reminder of the strength found in vulnerability and the importance of connection to our environment.

About the Artist

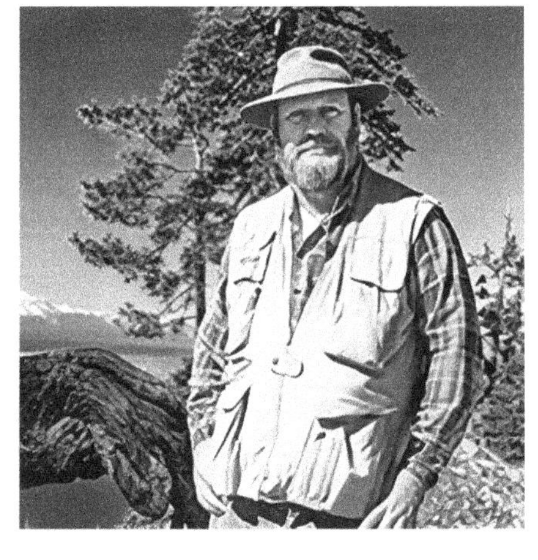

Dana Garrett is a service-disabled, retired Navy Chief Petty Officer whose lifelong passion for photography began with his first camera at age seven. Returning to active duty in 1999, after serving in the Air Force and Air Force Reserve for seven years and the Navy Reserve for 15 years, reignited Dana's commitment to the art, inspiring him to study photography seriously and refine his skills. Based in the scenic Virginia Range mountains near Reno, Nevada, Dana enjoys the tranquility of mountain living alongside his wife of 43 years and two beloved dogs.

Deeply connected to nature, Dana finds joy in capturing the outdoors through his lens. His interests are wide-ranging, encompassing landscapes, nature, astrophotography, night photography, abstract, macro, street, and architectural subjects. Dana's dedication to the craft extends beyond his own work; he has authored courses on the Fundamentals of Photography and Winter Photography, sharing his expertise with aspiring photographers.

Dana Garrett showcases his work and educational content on his YouTube channel, Pinyon Mountain Studios, and maintains an active presence on Instagram and Facebook under the same name. He has also been a participant in the annual month-long art festival in Reno called Artown and has shown his work in several business locations and galleries in California, Nevada, and Virginia. At The Artist's Gallery in Virginia, he went from being a member and maintenance man to being the Lighting Director and acting as an assistant curator. His artistic vision, shaped by years of experience and a genuine love for the natural world, shines through in every image he creates.

www.ingramcontent.com/pod-product-compliance
Lightning Source LLC
Chambersburg PA
CBHW042055030726
47602CB00003B/29